But Still My Child

LORETTA MILES TOLLEFSON

But Still My Child Copyright © 2013 Loretta Miles Tollefson

ISBN: 978-0-9983498-7-9

"They Call You Fetus" was published in *Digging for Roots:Dalmo'ma 5* in 1985

All rights reserved. No part of this book may be reproduced by any mechanical, photographic, or electronic process, or in the form of a phonographic recording; nor may it be stored in a retrieval system, transmitted or otherwise copied for public or private use (other than for "fair use" as brief quotations embodied in articles and reviews) without prior written permission.

Published by LLT Press, Eagle Nest, New Mexico

For the people who tried to tell me I wasn't alone but whose words were lost in my pain. I'm sorry it took me so long to understand what you were saying. Thank you.

Preface

Many years ago all my assumptions about how life should be: work I loved, marriage, children, etc—broke apart. I was newly married and pregnant. We were not rich, but we had each other and a baby coming. We were happy. And then I miscarried at five months. It still hurts to write these words, and it happened over thirty years ago.

The poems I wrote then helped me to survive. They were my lifeline during a time when I felt that no one else understood my pain, a pain I could not fully express except through the poems themselves.

It was only recently that I realized the pain I suffered wasn't unique. That sense of despair and loneliness, of feeling hopeless in the hands of an experience we cannot understand or control, is actually a normal reaction to the pain of pregnancy loss. I offer the poems I wrote then, and ones I've written more recently, as a small gift to you who are navigating this journey of sorrow.

I know that the poems in this collection cannot take away the pain or answer the questions that whirl through your mind as you cope with your sorrow. I hope that these expressions of my own pain will help you to feel that, although your pain is uniquely your own, others have also felt this anguish. You are not completely alone.

I will not insult your experience by telling you that it will make you stronger. I can tell you, though, that you are now a member of a larger fellowship of pain-carriers who have tapped into the reservoir of sorrow that undergirds the great joys of life. I can also tell you that the joys will come, although they may seem very distant at the moment. And that what you are experiencing now will flavor that joy and deepen it in a way you never thought possible.

On the page facing each poem is a section for you to record your thoughts, if that would be helpful to you. I have learned that writing out my thoughts, either in poetry or prose, helps me to process my pain. If this also works for you, I hope that you will use the "Your Thoughts" pages to put your feelings into words, and that doing so will ease your pain.

You have been plunged into a journey you did not ask for. I pray that this book helps to shed a little light on your path.

Loretta Miles Tollefson, Summer 2014

Contents

Upon a Miscarriage 3

They Call You Fetus 5

It Cannot Be 7

Alone 9

Time Has No Meaning... 11

The Dream 13

Fear 15

A Single Word 17

Barrenness 19

As Sharply As Sorrow 21

For Fear of Loss 23

Sunday Morning 25

You Never Suckled 27

Icy Waters 29

Compensations 32

Your Thoughts

Upon a Miscarriage
Spring 1983

They say I bear it well.
Death's done:
what's there to do but,
moving mutely to its beat,
continue on with life
and all the living, needing
round me?

They say I'll soon forget.
Heart knows:
the fruit,
however damaged by the frost,
is still the tree's.
She marks its drop.

Your Thoughts

They Call You Fetus
Spring 1983

They call you fetus.
Technical term for ligament, bone.
No ribbon tie of life or love
between us.

They call you dead.
"Fetal demise" packing away
long months of brooding, caring
into the attic.

You are these things.
Science will not brook denial
of its steel blue facts,
sharp as ice, unknowing.

You are all these,
and more:
my child,
my little one.

Your Thoughts

They Call You Fetus
Spring 1983

They call you fetus.
Technical term for ligament, bone.
No ribbon tie of life or love
between us.

They call you dead.
"Fetal demise" packing away
long months of brooding, caring
into the attic.

You are these things.
Science will not brook denial
of its steel blue facts,
sharp as ice, unknowing.

You are all these,
and more:
my child,
my little one.

Your Thoughts

It Cannot Be
Spring 1983

It cannot be that you would go
when only just begun;
that you would leave this earth of mine
your song as yet unsung.
A moment's hope the clothes you wore,
slight blossoming of love.
I cannot see beyond the dream
of holding you once more.

Your Thoughts

Alone
for Lowell, Spring 1983

I cannot face you.
Body curved into my burrow,
back taut against the world,
I stare into the void of my own emptiness
but cannot turn to question
whys
or wheres.
The ache too great to bear examination,
I crouch in my small corner,
sleeping past the tears
I fear to shed.

Your Thoughts

Time Has No Meaning
Spring 1983

Time has no meaning.
Before, behind,
above, below:
All movements unrelated

To this place I stand;
all pointless for the knowing
of this moment.
The compass points of purpose,
function
have no bearing on this instance,
space.
There is no world,
no being,
but where I am.

Your Thoughts

The Dream
Spring 1983

The dream,
so long entrenched,
mains fast within my soul
though all the outward surenesses,
so green with joy,
have crumbled once again
to bits of dried and dying leaves
brown from lack
of light:
the stubborn life
of hope.

Your Thoughts

Fear
Spring 1983

A lion tags my soul,
playing round the heels
of my emotions,
snapping at the laces of control,
weakening the knot
which keeps the feet from running.

This insidious menace--
cool and strong,
with facts unbending;
lithe and cruel,
with cold jaws snapping
at the ankles--
comes on unhurriedly
no matter how fast
I go.

Your Thoughts

A Single Word
Spring 1983

Pushed back into its proper corner,
held firm until it fills its usual space,
the fear seems small and insignificant,
without meaning, place.
But once a single word—
one lonely thought—
let into being
and it spreads
thick as dusky fog
to envelop every sphere created
and its creator, too.

Your Thoughts

Barrenness
for Toni, Fall 1984

Measure my love for you
by my silence,
by the words unspoken
that crowd to my lips,
by the smile only.
But do not look in my eyes
and do not ask that my throat
open in praise of the luck in your arms.
That's asking more than even a sister
can give.

Your Thoughts

As Sharply As Sorrow
Fall 1984

Joy pierces the heart
as sharply as sorrow.

You have felt its sure twisting
into your bones
though the knife's blade was for flowers
not wounds:
the spring of your cup
runneth over.

But the blue steel of sorrow's blade
has severed my flesh
and the wine of our merriment,
though of honey to you,
for me is edged richly
with pain.

Your Thoughts

For Fear of Loss
Fall 1985

My womb is made of lead.
It does not dare to feel
the warming touch of life
the egg so often promises—
sweet chirpings that would break its ice
into a mill of tears.
It will not hope to sense
more stirrings than its monthly own,
for fear of greater terror
than before.
For greater even than the grief of loss
is fear of loss
and all that it portends
again.

Your Thoughts

Sunday Morning

Brilliant smile,
cold hands,
eyes glancing into eyes
to further distances:
faces flash past
to say hello
and dance away again.
Promises only,
with nothing to fulfill.
Cold March sunshine.

Your Thoughts

You Never Suckled
Spring 2012

You never suckled at my breast, never
raised your eyes to mine, moving closer as
you turned a curve into my body. There
have been children since who have done so, yet
I have not forgotten the hope of you,
the stunned despair of your loss. Years have passed
since that searing emptiness, yet echoes
of pain still haunt my heart. Even now your
loss informs my joy in baby hands that
may yet reach toward me from your brothers' arms,
inflecting a sorrow I would shield them from.
If only I knew how.

Your Thoughts

Icy Waters
for Jim and Karen, Fall 2012

We are two lakes, high on the glacial slopes:
I, old as the hills surrounding us, you
young by mountain time. We lie beside each
other, reflecting the same events from
different angles, borders fringed by rock
and lichen, subject to storms that cannot
be controlled. I long to tell you how I've
withstood past weather, found strength to retain
apparent calm in face of winds so fierce
I thought they'd tear my soul apart. But mere
knowledge of my pain will not heal your heart.
No words I speak can sufficiently ease
the anguish that you feel. The ice of your
waters is yours alone. The waves lap most
fiercely now at your shores, not mine. Only
you can find within your depths the strength to
face the turmoil the storm roils up, to reach
for a wholeness that will not appear in

mere lightning time. My heart aches for the pain
you feel, my waters move in echoes of
your own, but I cannot stop your dark waves
from breaking. I can only reflect the
storm in my own way from shores that do not
touch your own, yet are shaped by the same event,
constrained forever by the rocks that bind us all.

Your Thoughts

Compensations
Summer 2013

After all this time, I still
look for reasons.
I'm told every event contains
a gift, a lesson gained; and that
even great sorrow can bring
joy, in the end.
It is not enough. I can not
find in these a just compensation.

Yes, the sorrow I felt then has tinged
the sweetness as I lifted
tiny arms to my own. The
memory of what
I endured softens my lips
as I strive to ease
the sadness in another's eyes. But
until the pain ceases
entirely, I will remain
unsatisfied, searching for answers
to questions I hardly know how to express,
pressing deeper

into territory I did not then
know existed, pausing only
to consider where next to turn.

Yet as I journey, I begin to feel
the search itself may be the reason
I seek: a prising wide of my quiescent heart, opening
to messages I would not
otherwise heed, exposing
the strong barriers I so unconsciously raise
against Spirit's movement.

How I long
for an easier way, a universe
in which the tool of anguish
lies rusty in a long forgotten shed,
covered by the lush green vines
of a landscape in which
dark questions are unneeded, where
I would find myself
turning quietly within
without the unexpected promptings
of sharp pain.

Your Thoughts

Your Thoughts

Your Thoughts

Your Thoughts

Your Thoughts

www.ingramcontent.com/pod-product-compliance
Lightning Source LLC
Chambersburg PA
CBHW030459010526
44118CB00011B/1010